Math·a·pedia

AUTHORS

Ricki Wortzman   David C. Brummett   Randall I. Charles

Lalie Harcourt   Carne S. Barnett   Brendan Kelly

CONTRIBUTING AUTHORS

Elisabeth Javor

Alma Ramirez

Freddie Lee Renfro

Mary M. Soniat-Thompson

Addison-Wesley Publishing Company
Menlo Park, California; Reading,
Massachusetts; New York;
Don Mills, Ontario; Wokingham,
England; Amsterdam; Bonn;
Paris; Milan; Madrid; Sydney;
Singapore; Tokyo; Seoul; Taipei;
Mexico City; San Juan

PRIMARY

Design: MKR Design, Inc.

Cover Design: The Pushpin Group

ISBN 0-201-84120-7

1 2 3 4 5 6 7 8 9 10 VH 98 97 96 95

TABLE of Contents

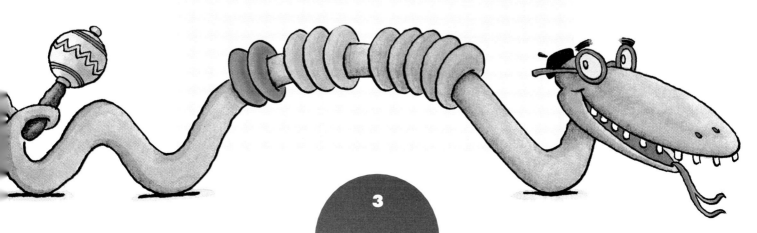

3

Add

We **add** to find out how many we have altogether.

Here are some adding situations.

I put two red hats. Now I will put three **more** yellow hats.

Can I **join** you? It looks like fun.

Oh my! Here comes **another one!**

We can use number sentences to tell about **adding**.

Here are number sentences that tell addition stories.

15 + 7 = 22

1 + 2 = 3

7 + 2 = 9

$$9 + 1 + 2 = 12$$

$$4 + 3 = 7$$

There are special names and symbols that we use when we talk about addition number sentences.

plus sign

sum

2 ⊕ 3 ⊜ 5

equal sign

There are many ways to think about adding.

7 and 5.
I know 7
and 3 make 10.
Then there are 2 more,
so that makes 12!

7 and 5.
That is the same
as 5 and 7,
and I know
that is 12!

7 and 5.
5 and 5 is 10,
so 7 and 5 is
10, 11, 12.

When we can't get answers in our heads, there are other **tools** to help us add.

We might use a **calculator.**

We might use the same **numbers of something** else.

23 + 48 = 71

We might use **groups of things** in numbers that are easier to count.

23 + 48 = 71

We might also use **pencil and paper**.

23 + 48 =

20 + 40 = 60

3 + 8 = 11

60 + 11 = 71

I can take the 20 in 23 and the 40 in 48 and add them. That is 60.

I still have 3 and 8 and that is 11.

I'll add 60 and 11 and that is 71.

I know 8 and 3 is 11. Since 11 is one ten and 1, I put the tens with the tens.

Now I've got 20 and 40 plus another 10 so that's 70.

```
  1
  23
+ 48
  71
```

The answer is 71.

Find out more about *adding* on page 84.

Alike

Things can be **alike** in many ways.

These grapes are alike.
They have the same shape.

They are different colors.

These oranges are alike.
They have the same shape
and color.

They are different sizes.

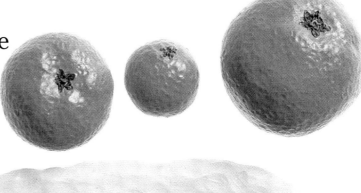

How are these **alike**?

How are these **different**?

Find out more about *alike* on pages 24 and 80.

Calculator

We can use calculators to do many things.

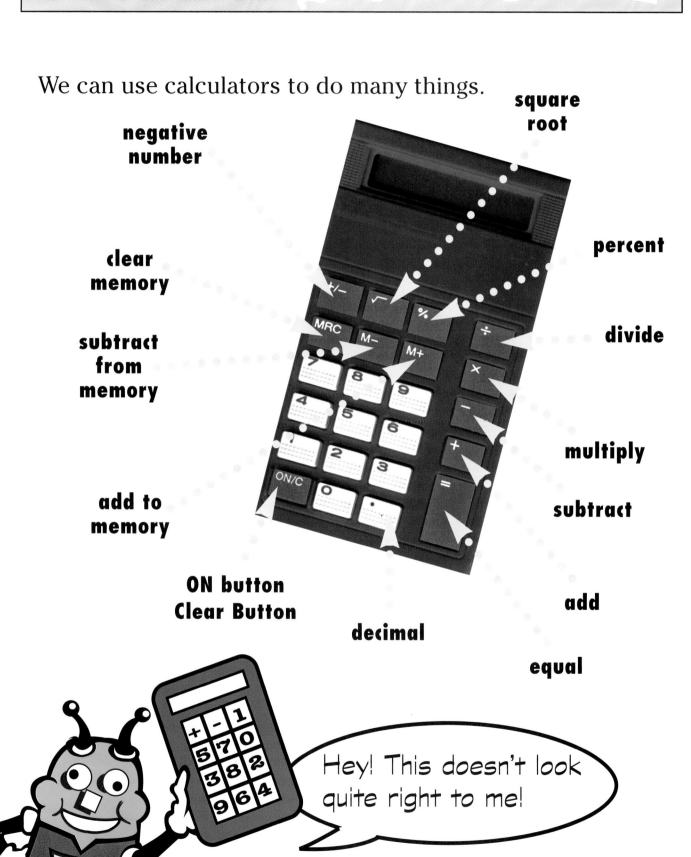

square root

negative number

percent

clear memory

subtract from memory

divide

multiply

subtract

add to memory

ON button
Clear Button

add

decimal

equal

Hey! This doesn't look quite right to me!

When we talk about things that might happen
we use words like: always, never,
likely, and unlikely.

Here are some things
that **always** happen.

The sun always sets.

A rabbit always hops.

This spinner will
always land in red.

Here are things that could **never** happen.

It never snows in the jungle.

A rabbit could never
fly a spaceship.

This spinner could never
land on yellow.

Here are things that are **likely** to happen.

It is likely to rain.

It is likely that this rabbit will eat the carrot.

It is likely that this spinner will land on blue.

Here are things that are **unlikely** to happen.

It is unlikely to snow today.

It is unlikely that a rabbit will go swimming.

It is unlikely that this spinner will land on pink.

18

Count

We count for many reasons.

We can count to find out **how many**.

> 1, 2, 3, 4, 5, 6

We can count to find out **how much**.

> $1, $2, $3, $4, $5

We can count to find out
how many more.
Or **how many less**.

WATER RIDES
$ 5

Boat Rental Rules
No More Than 4
No Less Than 2

Sometimes we **count on** or **count back**
to find out how many or how much.

We can count in many ways.

When we **skip count**, we use a **counting pattern**.

Here are some common skip-counting patterns.

By twos

2, 4, 6, 8, 10, 12, 14, 16, 18, 20

By fives

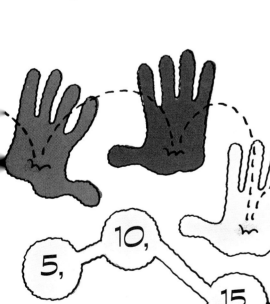

5, 10, 15, 20, 25, 30, 35,

10, 20, 30, 40, 50, 60, 70, 80, 90, 100

By tens

How should I count these?

40, 45, 50

How do you like to count?

Different

When we compare things, we talk about how they are alike and **different**.

Things can be different in many ways.

Here are different types of kites.
They are different shapes.
They are different colors.

These kites are different sizes.
But they are alike because they are all the same color and type.

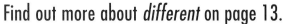

Find out more about *different* on page 13.

Digit

There are ten **digits**.

They are 0, 1, 2, 3, 4, 5, 6, 7, 8, 9.

A number is one or more digits.

Some
one-digit
numbers.

Some
two-digit
numbers.

Some
three-digit
numbers.

Can you find more numbers
for these groups?

Find out more about *digits* on pages 52–59.

Equal

We say groups are **equal** when they have the same number of things.

Our groups are **equal**. There are the same number of foxes as bears.

Our groups are not equal. There are **more** cats than dogs.

Eight is **greater than** six.

Equal Parts

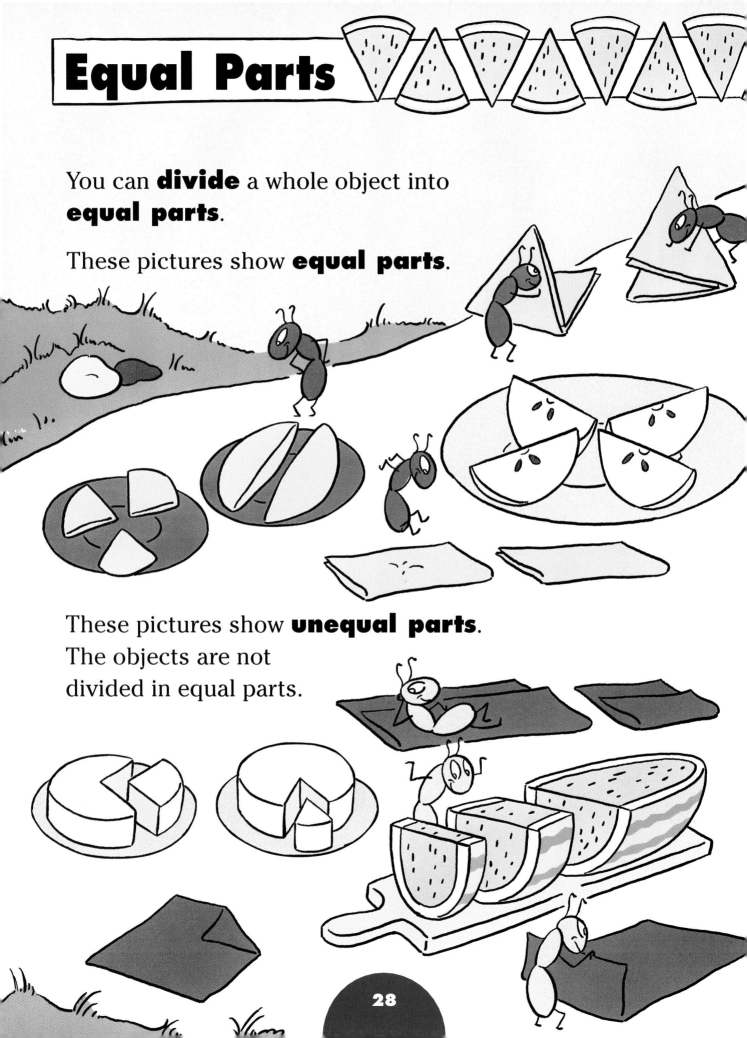

You can **divide** a whole object into **equal parts**.

These pictures show **equal parts**.

These pictures show **unequal parts**. The objects are not divided in equal parts.

You can also **divide** a collection of objects into **equal shares**.

These pictures show **equal shares.**

Here are **equal shares** and **leftovers.**

Find out more about *equal parts* and *shares* on page 26.

Estimate

We make an **estimate** when we tell how many or how much without actually counting or measuring. Sometimes we do not need to know an exact answer.

Even Numbers

Numbers are either even or odd.

Even numbers
of things make pairs.
There are **no leftovers**.

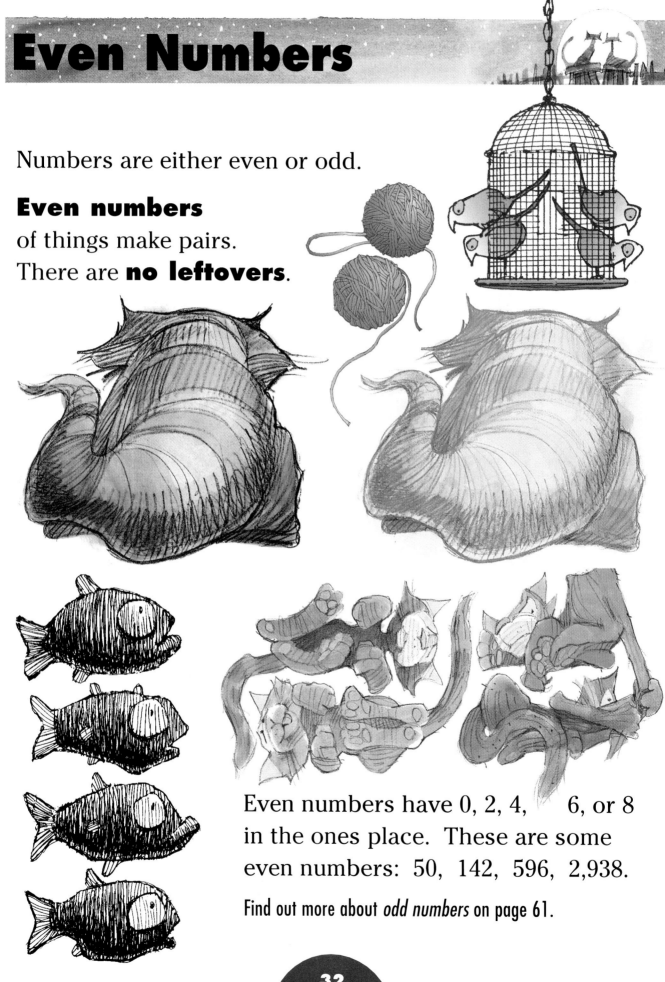

Even numbers have 0, 2, 4, 6, or 8 in the ones place. These are some even numbers: 50, 142, 596, 2,938.

Find out more about *odd numbers* on page 61.

Fractions

We can divide **whole objects** into equal parts that are called **fractions**.

1 whole sandwich

Here is a whole sandwich.

Now the sandwich is divided into **2** equal parts. Each part is called **one half.**

Here are some more things that are divided in **halves.**

$\frac{1}{2}$ of a sandwich

$\frac{1}{2}$ of a sandwich

When objects are divided into **4** equal parts we can say each part is **one quarter**. We can also call each part **one fourth** or $\frac{1}{4}$.

These are all divided into **quarters**.

$\frac{1}{4}$

$\frac{1}{4}$

$\frac{1}{4}$

$\frac{1}{4}$

These objects are divided into **3** equal parts. Each part is called **one third** or $\frac{1}{3}$. These are all divided into **thirds**.

$\frac{1}{3}$ $\frac{1}{3}$ $\frac{1}{3}$

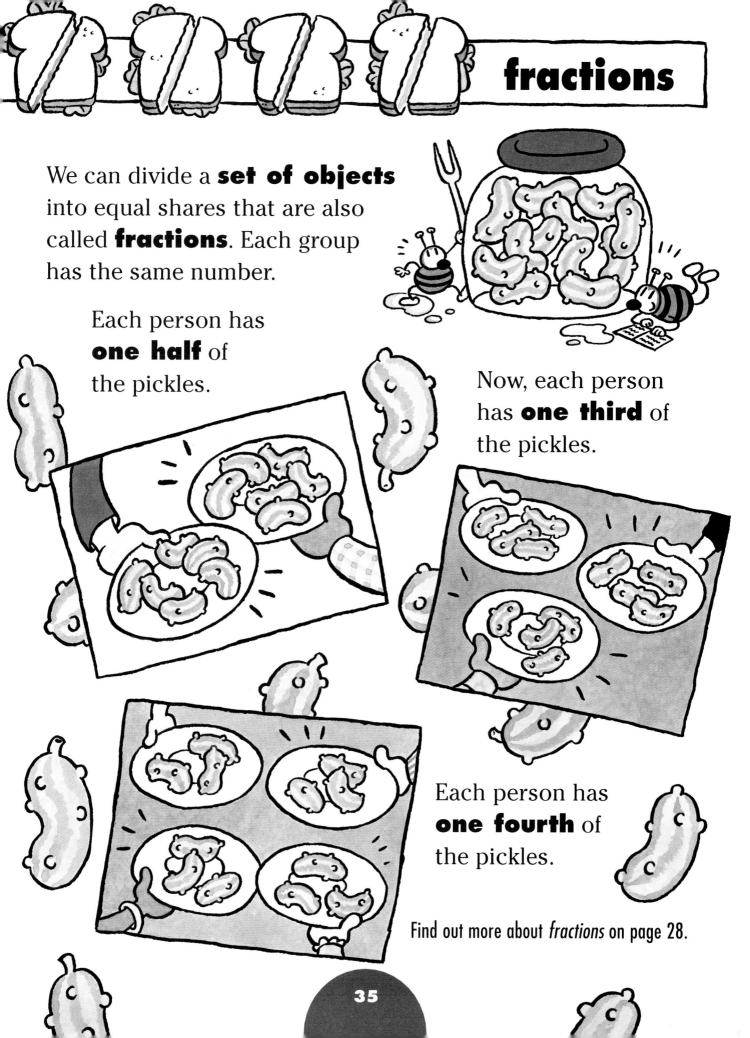

We can divide a **set of objects** into equal shares that are also called **fractions**. Each group has the same number.

Each person has **one half** of the pickles.

Now, each person has **one third** of the pickles.

Each person has **one fourth** of the pickles.

Find out more about *fractions* on page 28.

Graph

We use **graphs** to show information. Graphs help us see information at a glance.

There are many types of **graphs**.

Here are **real graphs**. They are made with real objects.

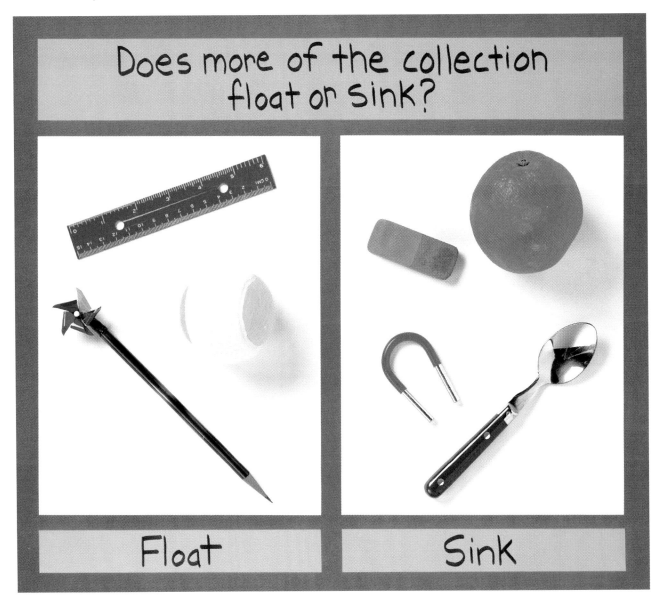

Does more of the collection float or sink?

Float

Sink

Walk   Bus   Car   Bike

How do you get to school?

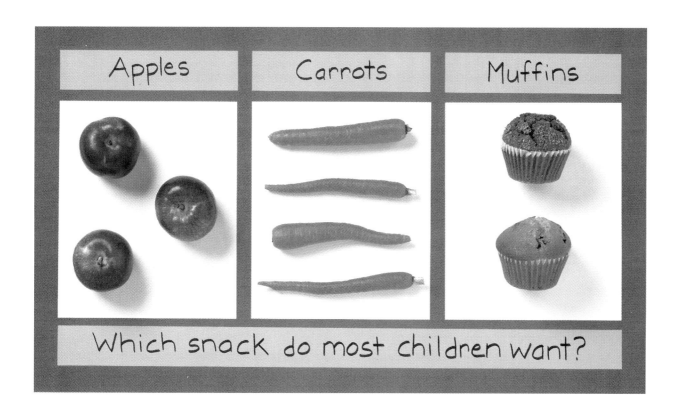

Apples   Carrots   Muffins

Which snack do most children want?

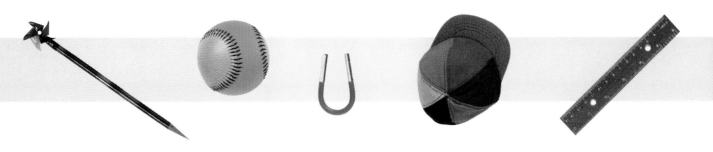

We can use pictures to make graphs. Picture graphs help us see information quickly.

Here are **picture graphs**.

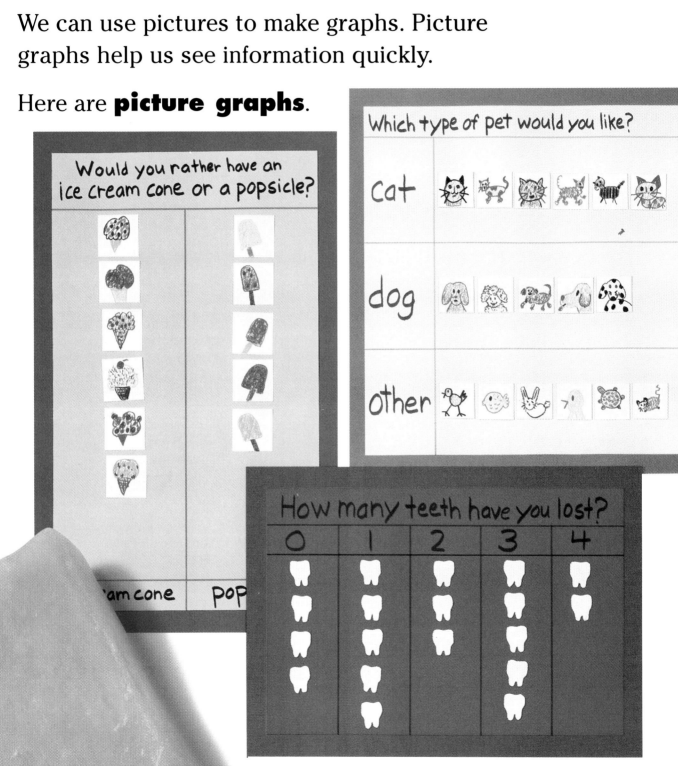

Would you rather have an ice cream cone or a popsicle?

...am cone   pop...

Which type of pet would you like?

cat

dog

other

How many teeth have you lost?

0	1	2	3	4

We can use squares or rectangles to make **bar graphs**. Bar graphs help us compare amounts quickly. Here are some **bar graphs**.

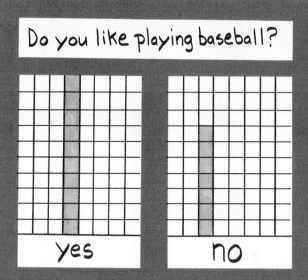

Do you like playing baseball?

yes   no

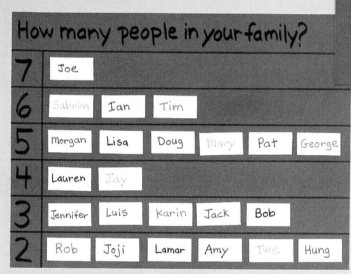

How many people in your family?

7	Joe					
6	Sabrina	Ian	Tim			
5	Morgan	Lisa	Doug	Mary	Pat	George
4	Lauren	Jay				
3	Jennifer	Luis	Karin	Jack	Bob	
2	Rob	Joji	Lamar	Amy	Twe	Hung

What is your favorite time of day?

morning	
afternoon	
night	

Location

Here are some words that tell us where things are **located**.

behind

on

beside

in front

Here are more words that tell us where things are **located**.

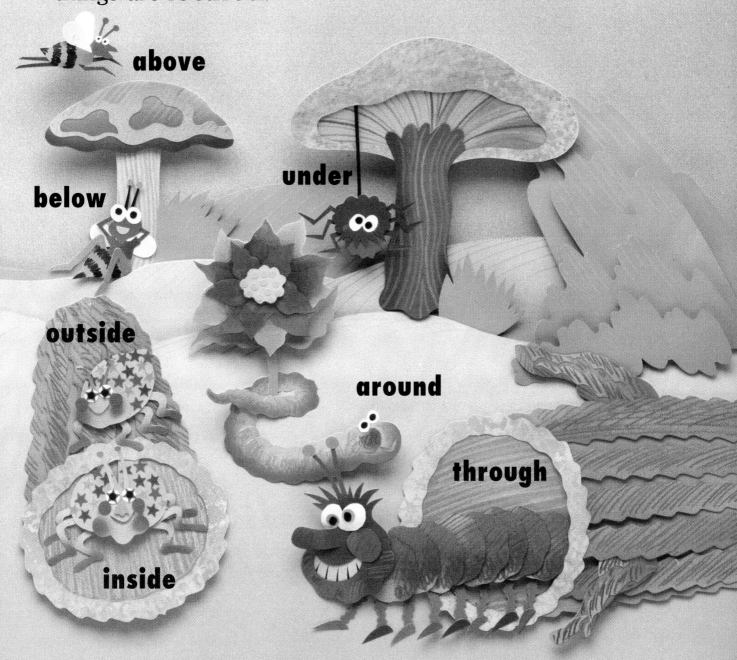

above

below

under

outside

around

through

inside

Find out more about *location* on page 42.

Map  64   6   19

A **map** is a picture that shows us where we can find things and places. When we look at a map we can see the shape of things from a bird's eye view.

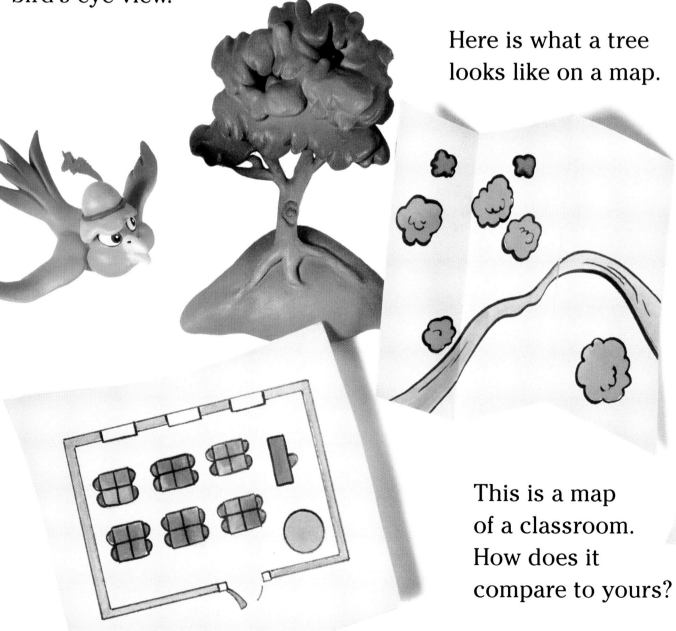

Here is what a tree looks like on a map.

This is a map of a classroom. How does it compare to yours?

This is a map that shows where places in a neighborhood are located.

This is a map that shows where places in the world are located.

Maps can also show us which **routes** we can
take to get places.

There are two routes to the treasure.
Which would you take?

START

Find out more about *where things are located* on page 40.

Measurement

There are many ways that we can **measure** people, objects and places to find out about them and to compare them.

We can measure to find the **distance** between people, objects or places.

length

width

height

JUST MARRIED

We can measure **length**, **width**, and **height** to find out the size of things.

We **weigh** things to find out how heavy things are or how they compare.

A pan balance can help us learn about how much things weigh.

lighter

heavier

Sometimes we measure the distance around something. This distance is called the **perimeter**.

Sometimes we measure the space that something covers. This space is called the **area**.

We can measure to find out how much something holds. We call this **capacity**.

empty

not full

full

47

MONSTER JUICE

We can measure things using
standard units. Standard units help us
tell other people about measurements.
The standard units on this page are called
customary units.

We can measure how long, wide,
tall, or far away something is using
units called **inches**, **feet**, and **yards**.

GUEST LIST

Wolfman

Frankenstein

Mummy

about one foot

one inch

A ruler can
measure in inches.
This bat has a
wingspan of five inches.

0   2   3   4   5

about one yard

We can measure how much something weighs using units called **pounds**.

one pound

FLOUR 1 lb

We can measure the capacity of containers using units called **cups**, **pints**, and **quarts**.

one cup

one pint

one quart

49

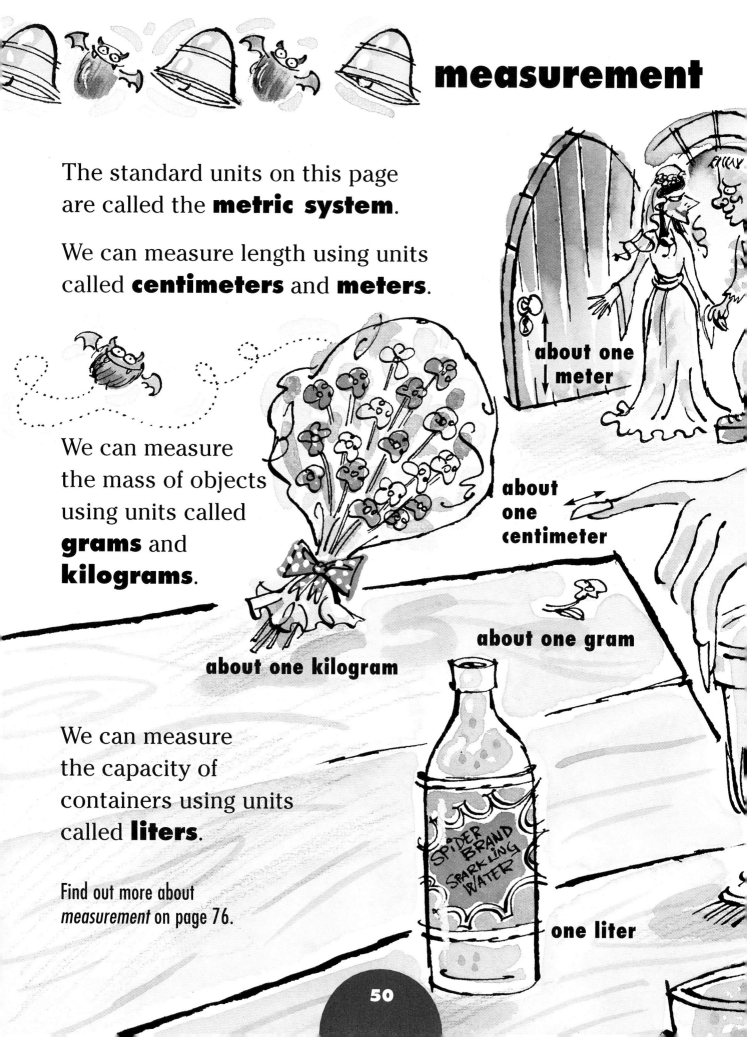

The standard units on this page are called the **metric system**.

We can measure length using units called **centimeters** and **meters**.

about one meter

We can measure the mass of objects using units called **grams** and **kilograms**.

about one centimeter

about one gram

about one kilogram

We can measure the capacity of containers using units called **liters**.

Find out more about *measurement* on page 76.

SPIDER BRAND SPARKLING WATER

one liter

Money

We use **money** to pay for things we buy. There are **coins** and **bills** worth different amounts.

Here are some different **coins**.

**penny
one cent
1¢**

**nickel
five cents
5¢**

**dime
ten cents
10¢**

**quarter
twenty-five cents
25¢**

**dollar bill
one dollar
$1**

**five dollar bill
five dollars
$5**

Why did the farmer feed money to his cows?

So he would get **rich** milk !

Number

Here are the **numbers** from one to ten.

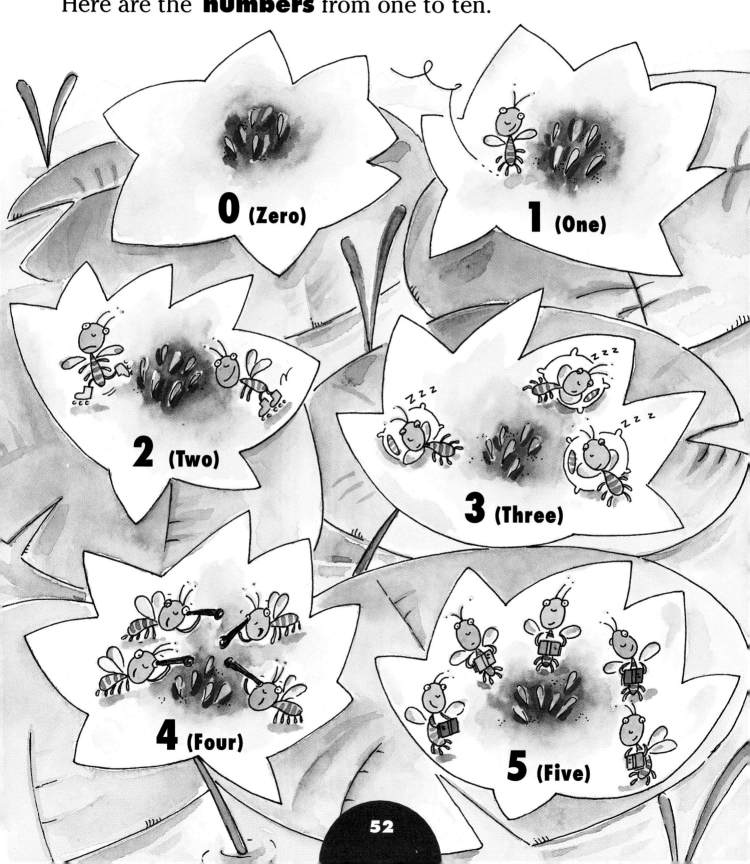

0 (Zero)

1 (One)

2 (Two)

3 (Three)

4 (Four)

5 (Five)

Here are the numbers
from 11 to 19.

11 (eleven)
10 and 1

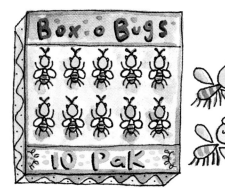

12 (twelve)
10 and 2

13 (thirteen)
10 and 3

14 (fourteen)
10 and 4

15 (fifteen)
10 and 5

16 (sixteen)
10 and 6

17 (seventeen)
10 and 7

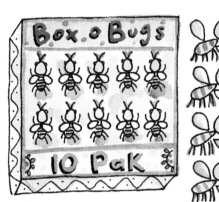

18 (eighteen)
10 and 8

19 (nineteen)
10 and 9

We say that two is company and three is a crowd. What's four and five?

Nine!

20 (twenty)

2 tens

30 (thirty)

3 tens

40 (forty)

4 tens

50 (fifty)

5 tens

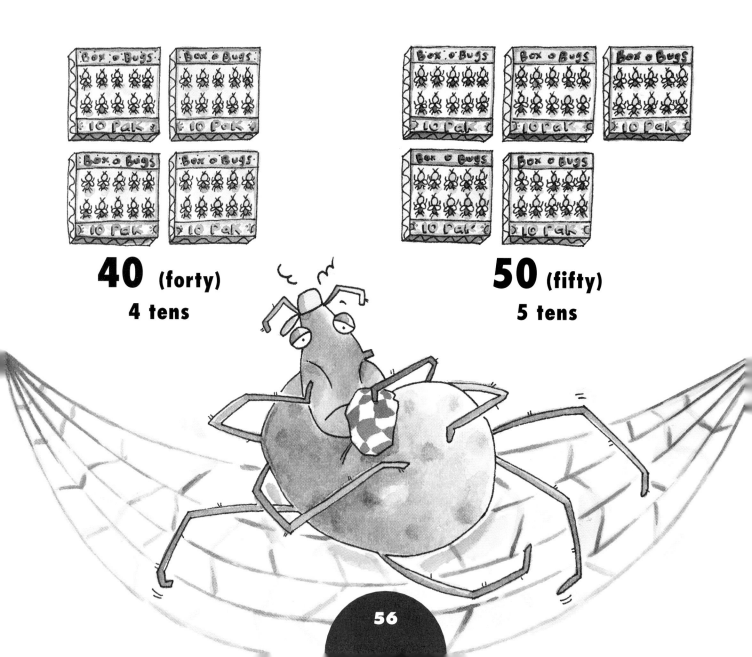

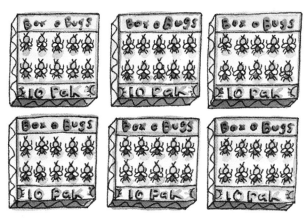

60 (sixty)

6 tens

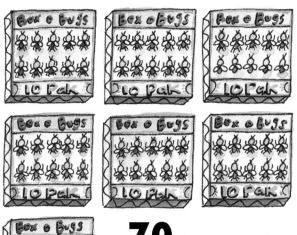

70 (seventy)

7 tens

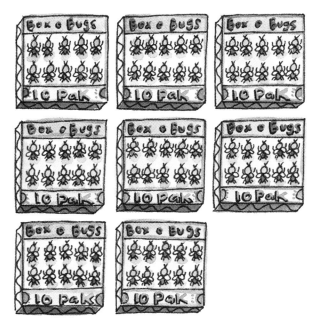

80 (eighty)

8 tens

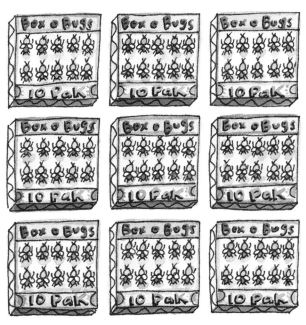

90 (ninety)

9 tens

Here is 100.

100
(one hundred)
10 tens

Here is 1000!

1000

(one thousand)
10 hundreds

Find out more about *numbers* on pages 19, 25, 32, 60, and 61.

Number Sentence

Number sentences use numbers, equal signs and other symbols.

Here are examples of **addition** number sentences.

plus   equals

$$2 + 5 = 7 \leftarrow \text{sum}$$

Here are examples of **subtraction** number sentences.

minus   equals

$$10 - 3 = 7 \leftarrow \text{difference}$$

You can use **addition and subtraction** in a number sentence.

$$5 + 3 - 2 = 6$$

Find out more about *number sentences* on pages 8–12 and 84–88.

Numbers are either odd or even.

Odd numbers

of things do not make pairs.
There are **leftovers**.

Odd numbers have 1, 3, 5, 7, or 9 in the
ones place. These are some odd numbers:
61, 43, 285, 647, 3,209.

Find out more about *even numbers* on page 32.

Order

Ordinal numbers are used to tell **order** or **position**.

Ordinal numbers can tell about your place in line.

King Kong Look

first	second	third	fourth	fifth	sixth
1st	2nd	3rd	4th	5th	6th

Ordinal numbers can tell you about the order people finished a race.

second
2nd

first
1st

third
3rd

order

We use ordinal numbers to name floors in buildings.

Alike Contest

fiftieth
50th

fortieth
40th

thirtieth
30th

twentieth
20th

seventh 7th   eighth 8th   ninth 9th   tenth 10th

tenth
10th

Today is May 7th

We use ordinal names to tell about dates.

When is first also last? ...In a line of one!

Pattern

We say something is a pattern when objects, events, or numbers **repeat**.

Each of these necklaces shows a pattern.

All of these pieces of cloth have patterns.

Sometimes we can have many different patterns.

What patterns do you see on this wall?

Some patterns grow.

What would come next?

Some events repeat over and over
to make patterns.

winter

spring

summer

fall

morning

noon

night

There are **number patterns** too.
Here are some patterns on an addition chart.

+	0	1	2	3	4	5
0	0	1	2	3	4	5
1	1	2	3	4	5	6
2	2	3	4	5	6	7
3	3	4	5	6	7	8
4	4	5	6	7	8	9
5	5	6	7	8	9	10

+	0	1	2	3	4	5
0	0	1	2	3	4	5
1	1	2	3	4	5	6
2	2	3	4	5	6	7
3	3	4	5	6	7	8
4	4	5	6	7	8	9
5	5	6	7	8	9	10

+	0	1	2	3	4	5
0	0	1	2	3	4	5
1	1	2	3	4	5	6
2	2	3	4	5	6	7
3	3	4	5	6	7	8
4	4	5	6	7	8	9
5	5	6	7	8	9	10

There are many more to find.

There are many different **counting patterns**. Here are some.

1, 2, 3, 4, 5, 6

2, 4, 6, 8, 10, 12

20, 40, 60, 80, 100

Shapes

Here are some **shapes**. When a shape is flat, we can call it a two-dimensional shape.

These are all **circles**.

When we draw lines from the center of a circle, they are all the same length.

What circles can you see around you?

Here are some **rectangles**.

All rectangles have
four sides and
four corners.

side →

corner →

The opposite sides
of a rectangle
have the same length.

What rectangles do you see around you?

Here are some **squares**.

All squares have four sides
and four corners.

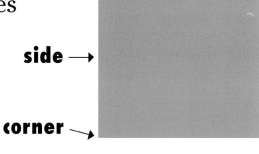

side →

corner →

Squares are special rectangles
because all sides of a square
are the same length.

What squares can you find around you?

Here are some **triangles**.

All triangles have three sides
and three corners.

side↘

corner→

About how many triangles do you think are in
this quilt? About how many squares?

73

The **pattern blocks** are different shapes.
Here is what they are called:

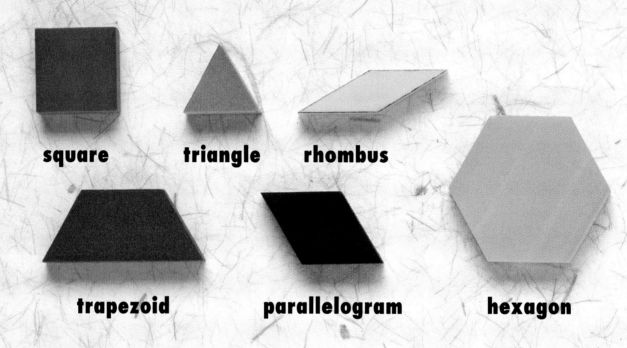

square   triangle   rhombus

trapezoid   parallelogram   hexagon

What shapes do you see?

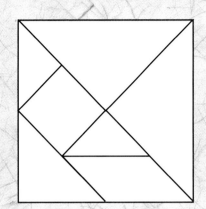

A puzzle called a **tangram** has seven shapes that can be put together to make a square.

There are many pictures we can make using the tangram pieces.

What shapes do you see in me?

Find out more about *shapes* on page 71.

Size

There are many words that help us tell about **size**.

tall

taller

tallest

short

shorter

shortest

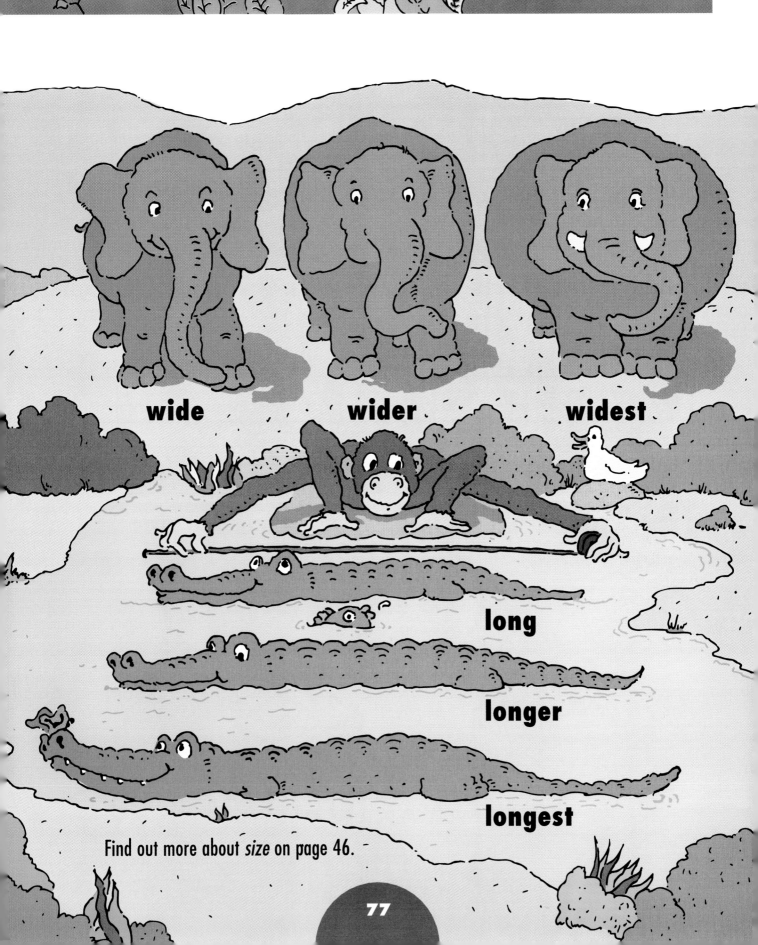

wide   wider   widest

long

longer

longest

Find out more about *size* on page 46.

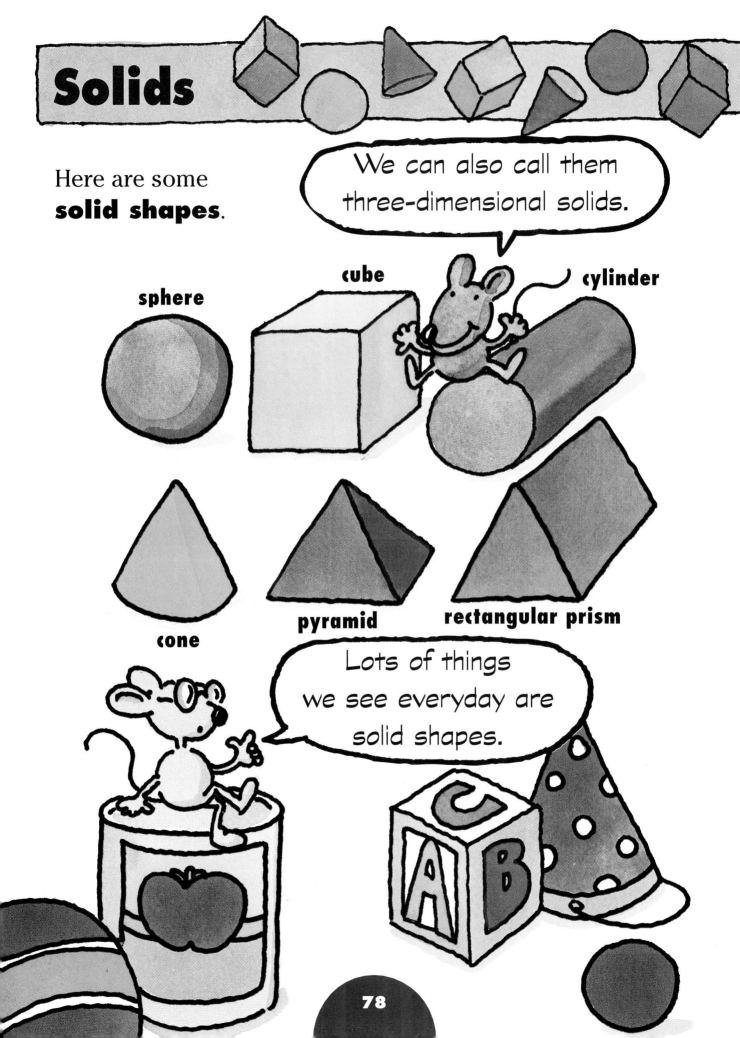

Solids

Here are some **solid shapes**.

We can also call them three-dimensional solids.

sphere

cube

cylinder

cone

pyramid

rectangular prism

Lots of things we see everyday are solid shapes.

solids

Here are some words that help us talk about solids.

corner

edge

face

We can make shapes using solids.

Find out more about *shapes* on page 70.

Sort

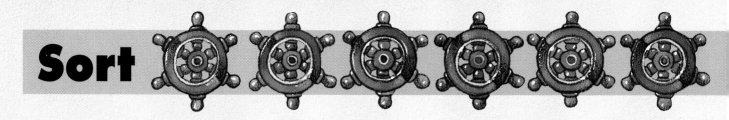

We **sort** when we put like things into groups.

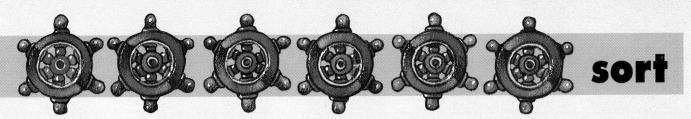

We can usually sort collections in many ways.

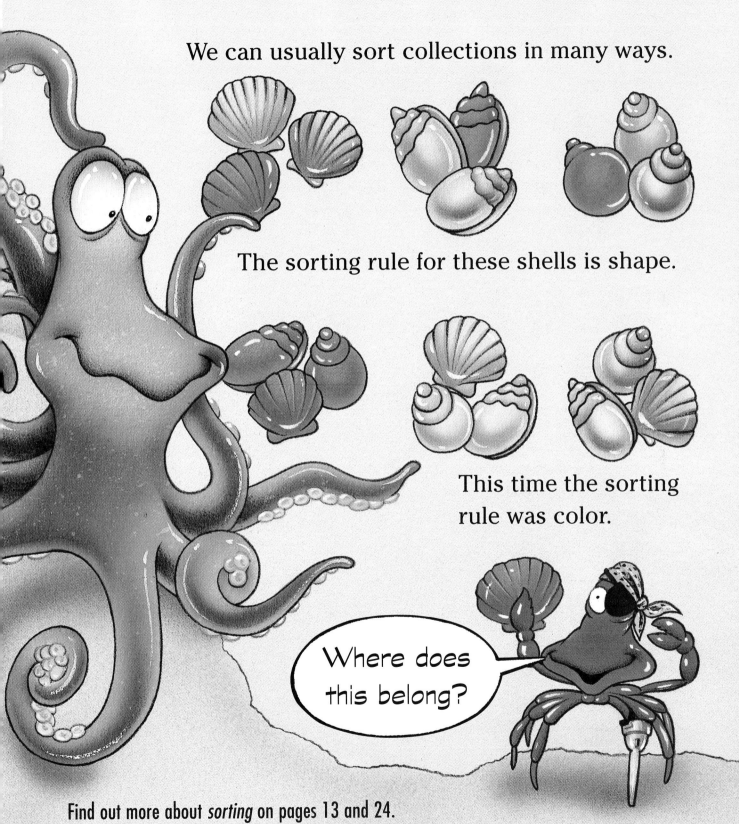

The sorting rule for these shells is shape.

This time the sorting rule was color.

Where does this belong?

Find out more about *sorting* on pages 13 and 24.

Subtract

We **subtract** to find out how many are left when some things are taken away. We subtract to find a missing number. We subtract when we compare numbers.

Here are some subtracting situations.

These look so good! I think I'll take a few **away** with me.

Oh no! There goes **another one.**

Here, I'll give you this one. That's **one less** for me.

HIT A DOLL AND TAKE IT HOME

We can use number sentences to tell about **subtracting**.

Here are number sentences that tell subtraction stories.

3 - 1 = 2

8 - 5 = 3

12 - 3 = 9

There are special names and symbols that we use when we talk about subtraction number sentences.

minus sign

equal sign

7 - 3 = 4

difference

There are a lot of ways to think about subtracting.

11 take away 3. That's 11, 10, 9, 8!

11 take away 3. Hmm, I know that 8 and 3 is 11, so that means 11 take away 3 is 8.

11 take away 3. I can take away 1. That leaves 10, and then 10 take away 2 is 8!

FLEA CIRCUS

When we can't get answers in our heads, there are other **tools** to help us subtract.

We might use a **calculator**.

23 - 14 =

23 - 14 = 9

We might **count** 23 then take 14 away.

We might **group things** in tens and then subtract.

23 - 14 = 9

subtract

We might also use **pencil and paper**.

> I can think
> 14 is 10 and 4.
> Then 23 minus 10,
> that's 13.

23 - 14 =

23 - 10 = 13

13 - 4 = 9

> I still have
> 4 left from 14.
> So 13 minus 4 is 9.
> The answer is 9.

> I can't take 4 away from 3,
> so I'm going to write 23
> as 1 ten and 13 ones.

> Now, I can take 4 from 13
> and that is 9.

$$\begin{array}{r} 1\ \ 13 \\ 2\ \ \cancel{3} \\ -\ 1\ \ 4 \\ \hline 9 \end{array}$$

Find out more about *subtracting*
on page 60.

> Ten from 10 is 0.
> My answer is 9.

We can do a survey using an **interview**. An interview is a planned set of questions that we ask someone.

What is your nest made of?

How many chicks in your family?

Do you live in a birdhouse or a people house?

We can do a survey using a **questionnaire**. A questionnaire is a collection of questions people write answers to.

Your Name ____
How old are you? ____
Are you male or female? ____
What kind of bird are you? ____

Find out more about *surveys* on pages 36 and 91.

Tally

A **tally** is a way to keep track of counting. Tally marks are made in groups of five like this: ||||

We can count tally marks quickly. Here are some ways we can use tally marks.

Our spinner results:

red |||| ||||

yellow |||| |||| |

What is your favorite Ice cream flavor?

Vanilla |||| |||| ||

Chocolate |||| |

Bubble Gum |||| |||| |||| |

Rocky Road ||||

Clocks and **calendars** help us measure **time**.

We can read a clock to tell when it is time to wake up.

Each page on a calendar shows us the days of a **month**. There are seven days in a **week**.

Sunday	Monday	Tuesday	Wednesday	Thursday	Friday	Saturday
1	2	3	4	5	6	7
8	9	10	11	12	13	14

There are 12 **months** in a year.

We use **clocks** to tell the time.

There are 60 **seconds** in one **minute**.

There are 60 **minutes** in one **hour**.

There are 24 **hours** in a day.

minute hand

hour hand

8:00 a.m.
eight o'clock

12:30 p.m.
twelve-thirty
or half-past-twelve

3:45 p.m.
three-forty-five
or quarter-to-four

8:10 p.m.
eight-ten or
ten-past-eight

Index

Acknowledgments

Illustration

Tim Haggerty: 6-12
Obadinah Heavner: 13
Julie Pace: 14
Jim Paillot: 15-18
Stan Tusan: 19-23
Sally Jo Vitsky: 24
Sinclair Seibert: 25
Randy Verougstraete: 26-27
Phil Marden: 28-29
Stephen Schudlich: 30-31
Stephen Foster: 32
David Brion: 33-35
Leo Monahan: 40-41
Jack Graham: 42-45
R. Barnes Murphy: 46-50
Eric Lodde: 51
Luisa D'Augusta: 52-59
Paul Ratz de Tagyos: 60
Stephen Foster: 61
Steve McInturff: 62-63
Alex Bloch: 64-69
Valerie Fedun: 73
Myron Grossman: 76-77
Kimble Mead: 78-79
Jean Pidgeon: 80-81
Debbie Tilley: 82-88
Tim Haggerty: 89-90
Liisa Chauncy Guida: 91
Lionel Kalish: 92-93

Photography

Photo Management: **Picture It Corporation**
Clara Aich: 36-39, 70-75